THE ABBOTT CREEK
COOK BOOK

———  ———

Amish Sweet Shop books by Naomi Miller

Blueberry Cupcake Mystery
Christmas Cookie Mystery
Lemon Tart Mystery
Pumpkin Pie Mystery
Chocolate Truffle Mystery
Peach Cobbler Mystery

Windy Gap Wishes

A Mother for Leah
A Suitor for Rebekah

Plain Fairy Tales

Ashes to Amish
Her Beastly Blessing

Children's Books

Sophie Finds a Family
Sophie Celebrates Thanksgiving
Sophie's New Home

The Abbott Creek Cook Book

Naomi Miller

*Dedicated to my faithful readers,
and to everyone out there who knows
how to appreciate the sweet things in life.*

Copyright © Naomi Miller 2019
The Abbott Creek Cook Book

S&G Publishing
Knoxville TN 37950

The Abbott Creek Cook Book / Naomi Miller
ISBN: 978-1948733281

All rights reserved. No part of this publication may be reproduced or transmitted for commercial purposes, without written permission of the publisher, except for brief quotations in printed reviews. Scripture quotations are from the Holy Bible (KJV)

This book is a work of fiction. Names, characters, places, and incidents are either products of the author's imagination or used fictitiously. Any similarity to actual people, organizations, and/or events is purely coincidental

Cover, graphics and formatting by Expresso Designs

Second edition 2024

Contents

Blueberry Cupcake Mystery *excerpt* — 1
- Katie's Blueberry Cupcakes — 3
- Blueberry Coffee Cake — 4
- Blueberry-Lemon Muffins — 5
- Blueberry Cheesecake Squares — 6
- Chocolate Chip Cookies — 7
- Peanut Butter Cookies — 8
- Banana Bread — 9
- Zucchini Bread — 10
- Cranberry Bread — 11
- Fresh Fruit Salad — 12
- Gwen's Veggie Casserole — 13
- Berry Smoothie Drink — 14

Christmas Cookie Mystery *excerpt* — 15
- Frosted Christmas Cookies — 17
- Ginger Snap Cookies — 19
- Irish Shortbread Cookies — 20
- Pecan Drop Cookies — 21
- Christmas Date Cookies — 22
- Gingerbread Cookies — 23
- Holiday Snickerdoodles — 24
- Christmas Fudge — 25
- Salted Caramel Peanut Butter Kisses — 26
- Festive Sugar Cookies — 27
- Irish Gingerbread Cookies — 28
- Irish Salted Chocolate Cookies — 30

Lemon Tart Mystery *excerpt* — 33
- Katie's Triple Lemon Cookies — 35
- Lemon Surprise Cupcakes — 36
- Katie's Lemon Tarts — 37
- Zesty Lemon Bars — 38
- Singing Night Lemonade — 40
- Orange Supreme Bliss Bars — 41
- Katie's Lemon Bars — 42
- Luscious Lemon Pie — 43
- Katie's Pie Crust — 44
- Easy Pineapple Upside Down Cake — 45
- Katie's Egg Custard Pie — 46
- Emma's Homemade Egg Salad — 47

Pumpkin Pie Mystery *excerpt* — 49

- Rachel's Pumpkin Pie — 51
- Rachel's Sweet Potato Pie — 52
- Naomi's Honey Butter — 53
- Naomi's Roasted Turkey — 54
- Naomi's Holiday Chex Mix — 55
- Iva's Cornbread Dressing — 56
- Rachel's Pumpkin Bread — 57
- Cranberry Pumpkin Bread — 58
- Martha's Sausage Balls — 59
- Rachel's Sweet Potato Casserole — 60
- Pumpkin Pecan Pancakes — 61
- Pumpkin Orange Cookies — 62

Chocolate Truffle Mystery *excerpt* — 63

- Katie's Triple Chocolate Cake — 65
- Andrew's Banana Bread — 66
- Katie's Chocolate Truffles — 67
- Iva's Red Velvet Cake — 68
- Iva's Cream Cheese Frosting — 69
- Katie's Super Hot Chocolate — 70
- Katie's Never Fail Fudge — 71
- Ohio's Buckeye Candy — 72
- Martha's Cream Cheese Fudge — 73
- Andrew's Favorite Church Cake — 74
- Iva's Pecan Pie — 75
- Naomi's Favorite Caramel Bars — 76

Peach Cobbler Mystery *excerpt* — 77

- Katie's Peach Cobbler — 79
- Katie's Baby Shower Mints — 80
- Katie's Party Mints — 81
- Gwen's Baby Shower Cupcakes — 82
- Katie's Peach Punch — 83
- Peanut Butter Krispie Treats — 84
- Katie's Rice Pudding — 85
- Martha's Cooked Apples — 86
- Naomi's 7-Layer Salad — 87
- Naomi's Honey Mustard — 88
- Naomi's Garlic Herb Spread — 89
- Amish Wedding Broccoli Cheese Soup — 90

Introduction

This has been such an awesome journey for me... It's one that I really didn't plan, but when my publisher suggested that I write this cookbook, I agreed that it would be a great way to bring the Amish Sweet Shop Mystery series together... and make it even better!

Since the very first Amish Sweet Shop Mystery story, my readers have asked if I would be writing a cookbook to go along with the series. At the time, the idea seemed impossible, and for a long time, even though readers continued to ask for one, I pushed the idea to the back-burner. Finally my publisher asked me to make time. We sat down and worked out all the details and it wasn't nearly as hard as I expected it to be. The hardest part was definitely trying to resist all the delicious desserts (I have diabetes, so a bite or two from each recipe was all I could have).

In the meantime, we are working together to update the six books in the series. Next year the 2nd edition of each book will be releasing – with a few additional recipes.

Christmas Cookie Mystery will remain the same, with twelve recipes. The other five books will each have six recipes. This cookbook will include all of the recipes, with an additional six recipes for the five books, for a total of seventy-two delicious recipes. And we have included some brand new recipes for the rest of the series... giving each book a total of twelve recipes. Seventy-two recipes... most of them are desserts, but I included some family favorites.

    I hope you enjoy this cookbook as much as I enjoyed writing it. As I worked through it, I enjoyed revisiting each Sweet Shop story and the wonderful people of Abbott Creek. I lost my mother when I was eighteen. I wanted to honor her and this gave me the perfect chance to do so, by including several of her favorite recipes here. Try them; I think you'll love them.

Blessings to you all,
Naomi

And be ye kind one to another, tenderhearted, forgiving one another, even as God for Christ's sake hath forgiven you.

- Ephesians 4:32

Blueberry Cupcake Mystery

Katie Chupp felt a chill run through her as she unlocked the door to The Sweet Shop. Hesitating, she turned and looked around, taking in the scenery around her. around her.

It didn't seem possible that the feeling had anything to do with her surroundings. The day was just beginning and it looked as if it was going to be a beautiful day.

The blue sky was pleasant to behold, with white, fluffy clouds lazily floating by, the sun already shining brightly, and a warm breeze gently wafting around her. Up and down the street, American flags were waving in the breeze, heralding the festivities. Red, white and blue decorations were in all the store windows.

The town was ready to celebrate Independence Day.

Katie anxiously awaited the fireworks that would be set off tonight, under cover of darkness. She was looking forward to sitting on a blanket with her family, watching as the fireworks exploded high in the sky.

The Fourth of July was one of her favorite holidays. Everyone met at the town square to celebrate. Many of the families, including Katie's, would eat a late supper while waiting for the fireworks.

Katie had no time to waste—yet she waited, sensing that something was wrong. She couldn't imagine what it could be, to cause such a reaction. It made no sense to her.

The Sweet Shop would be busy today. Extra baking had been done during the past few days, in preparation of the holiday. Lots of customers would be coming into the bakery to pick up their orders today. Her thoughts shifted to the long list of tasks that must be completed each day to prepare for customers. There was much to be done. There would be no time to rest once the bakery opened.

With a silent prayer of thanks for such a beautiful day, Katie stepped inside the bakery.

KATIE'S BLUEBERRY CUPCAKES

CUPCAKES

1	white cake mix
2 cups	fresh blueberries
3 large	eggs
1/3 cup	oil
1 1/3 cups	water

Prepare cake mix according to directions. Add 2 cups of fresh blueberries and fold into batter. Bake following the instructions on the cake mix box.

ICING

1 cup	confectioner's sugar
2 tablespoons	whole milk (plus additional milk as needed)

Prepare icing, mixing small amounts of confectioners sugar with milk to desired consistency. Spread onto cooled cupcakes.

Katie bakes dozens of blueberry cupcakes every year for the July 4th celebration at the town square. Wrapped in blue paper liners with shiny stars, these cupcakes are a favorite snack for Bobby Davis and his brothers.

BLUEBERRY COFFEE CAKE

CAKE

3 cups	self-rising flour
2-3 tablespoons	all-purpose flour
3 cups	fresh blueberries
2 large	eggs
1 cup	unsalted butter
1 cup	white sugar
1 cup	whole milk

Katie suggests serving hot coffee with each slice of coffee cake, but Bobby Davis prefers his with a scoop of vanilla ice cream for a tasty treat.

Preheat oven to 375°F. Cream together softened butter and sugar in a large bowl. Beat egg in a small bowl, then add to the butter and sugar mixture. Add 3 cups of flour to the mixture, 1 cup at a time, mixing slowly.

Place blueberries in clean bowl and dust lightly with the flour. Shake gently, covering blueberries with the flour. Gently fold the blueberries into the mixture. Pour batter into 2 greased and floured 8" baking dishes.

TOPPING

6 tablespoons	unsalted butter
1/2 cup	self-rising flour
1/2 cup	white sugar
1 teaspoon	cinnamon

Prepare the topping, mixing flour, sugar, and cinnamon in a bowl. Cut in slices of butter until mixture is crumbly. Spread topping over the batter and bake 45 minutes or until golden brown.

BLUEBERRY-LEMON MUFFINS

4 cups	self-rising flour
3 tablespoons	all-purpose flour
2 1/2 cup	fresh blueberries
2 large	eggs
1 1/2 sticks	unsalted butter
1 cup	sour cream
1 cup	white sugar
1 cup	whole milk
2 teaspoons	grated lemon peel
4 teaspoons	lemon juice

Preheat oven to 400°F. Combine 4 cups of flour and sugar in a large bowl. Using whisk, mix egg, butter, sour cream, milk, lemon peel and lemon juice in a large bowl. Add flour mixture and mix until moistened.

Place blueberries in clean bowl and dust lightly with 3 tablespoons of flour. Shake gently, covering blueberries with the flour. Gently fold blueberries into mixture.

Line cupcake pan(s) with paper liners. Carefully spoon batter into cupcake liners. Bake 25 minutes or until golden brown.

Place muffins on wire rack to cool.

Recipe makes 24 muffins.

Katie often bakes these for her boyfriend Travis, since he's very fond of lemony treats.

BLUEBERRY CHEESECAKE SQUARES

CUPCAKES

1 package	bakery style blueberry muffin mix
1/2 cup	unsalted butter
1/3 cup	crushed pecans
8oz package	cream cheese
1 large	egg
1/2 cup	white sugar
1 teaspoon	grated lemon peel
3 tablespoons	lemon juice

Preheat oven to 350°F. Grease 9" square pan.

In a medium size bowl, combine muffin mix and butter, using pastry blender to mix thoroughly. Add crushed pecans to mixture. Press mixture into bottom of pan. Bake 15 minutes.

In another bowl, combine softened cream cheese and sugar, beating until smooth. Add the egg, lemon peel and lemon juice, beating until mixed well. Spread over the baked mixture in the pan. Sprinkle blueberries over the top, then sprinkle topping packet from the muffin mix over the blueberries. Bake another 35 minutes or until the filling is set.

Cool. Refrigerate until ready to serve.

CHOCOLATE CHIP COOKIES

2/3 cup	unsalted butter
1/2 cup	white sugar
1/2 cup	brown sugar
1 large	egg
1 3/4 cups	self-rising flour
1 1/4 cups	semi-sweet chocolate chips

Preheat oven to 375°F. In a large bowl, combine butter, white sugar, brown sugar, and egg. Slowly add flour until well mixed. Fold in chocolate chips.

Drop rounded teaspoons of dough about 2" apart on uncreased baking sheet. Bake 8-10 minutes or until delicately browned (cookies should still be soft).

Cool slightly before transferring cookie from baking sheet to wire racks.

PEANUT BUTTER COOKIES

1 cup	peanut butter
1 cup	brown sugar
1 stick	unsalted butter
1 tablespoon	pure vanilla extract
3 tablespoons	whole milk
1 large	egg
1 3/4 cups	self-rising flour

Preheat oven to 375°F. In a large bowl, combine peanut butter, brown sugar, butter, vanilla and milk. Using mixer, beat on medium speed until well blended. Add egg. Slowly add flour and mix at low speed just until blended.

Drop rounded teaspoons of dough about 2" apart on uncreased baking sheet. If desired, use a fork to create crisscross pattern on each cookie.

Bake 7 minutes or until dough is set (be careful not to over-bake cookies).

Cool slightly before transferring cookies from baking sheet to wire racks.

BANANA BREAD

4	bananas, sliced
2 cups	self-rising flour
2 large	eggs
3/4 cup	white sugar
2 sticks	unsalted butter
1 teaspoon	pure vanilla extract

Preheat oven to 350°F. Mash bananas in a large bowl. Add eggs and vanilla and mix together. Add dry ingredients. Mix thoroughly.

Pour mixture into greased loaf pan. Bake 50-60 minutes or until golden brown.

Katie doesn't often snack while she's baking, but occasionally, when she's getting ready to leave, she'll wrap up a few slices of banana bread to enjoy later. Although it isn't mentioned in these six books, banana bread is one of Katie's favorite treats.

> *Katie doesn't often snack while she's baking, but occasionally, when she's getting ready to leave, she'll wrap up a few slices of banana bread to enjoy later. Although it isn't mentioned in these six books, banana bread is one of Katie's favorite treats.*

ZUCCHINI BREAD

3 large	eggs
2 cups	brown sugar
2 sticks	unsalted butter
3 teaspoons	pure vanilla extract
3 cups	self-rising flour
1 teaspoon	ground cinnamon
3/4 teaspoon	tsp ground cloves
1 cup	chopped nuts
1 cup	crushed pineapple, drained

Preheat oven to 350°F. Beat the eggs. Add sugar, butter and vanilla; mix well. Grate zucchini. Stir into mixture. Add flour, cinnamon and cloves and stir. Add chopped nuts and pineapple. Mix well.

Pour mixture into 2 greased loaf pans. Bake 50-60 minutes or until golden brown.

CRANBERRY BREAD

1 cup	cranberries, chopped
1 tablespoon	grated orange peel
3/4 cup	orange juice
1 cup	white sugar
1 tablespoon	olive oil
1 large	egg, beaten
2 cups	self-rising flour

Mix together flour and sugar. Add oil. Stir in orange juice, egg and grated orange peel, mixing just enough to moisten. Fold in cranberries and nuts.

Preheat oven to 350° F. Pour mixture into greased and floured loaf pan. Bake 50-60 minutes or until golden brown. Cool on wire rack for 15-20 minutes before removing from pan.

FRESH FRUIT SALAD

SALAD

2	golden delicious apples
1 cup	assorted berries
3	bananas, sliced
1 cup	pineapple chunks
1 can	fruit cocktail

Cut apple into small chunks. Add apple chunks, grapes, banana slices, pineapple chunks and fruit cocktail.

DRESSING

1/2 cup	sour cream
1 cup	vanilla yogurt
1 tablespoon	raw honey
1 teaspoon	lime juice
1 cup	crushed ice

Combine sour cream and vanilla yogurt. Mix well, then add raw honey and lime juice. Add ice and stir. Gently combine with fruit. Serve cold.

Katie brings her favorite fruit salad to work at least once a week to share with her co-workers. Since she and the others are surrounded by all sorts of treats, the fruit salad is a great snack to have close by.

GWEN'S VEGGIE CASSEROLE

32 ounces	*frozen vegetables*
1 stick	*unsalted butter*
8 ounces	*Velvetta cheese, cubed*
1 sleeve	*Ritz crackers*

Preheat oven to 325°F. Cut cheese into cubes and set aside. Prepare frozen vegetables according to directions, then drain. Place 1/2 of the vegetables in a large casserole dish. Melt cheese cubes with 1/2 stick of butter. Pour 1/2 of the cheese sauce over the vegetables. Place the rest of the vegetables in the casserole dish and pour remaining cheese sauce over vegetables.

Crush the crackers before opening the pack. Melt 1/2 stick of butter. Add crushed crackers and sprinkle over the vegetables.

Bake uncovered 20-25 minutes or until golden brown. Serve warm.

Katie taught Gwen how to make this delicious, yet nourishing dish. Gwen was eager to learn how to prepare a few meals for her family and asked for Katie's help so she could surprise her mom and brothers. Apparently the cheese and crackers were the perfect thing to hide the healthy vegetables because Gwen's brothers gobble up every bite whenever she makes it.

BERRY SMOOTHIE DRINK

1 cup	blueberries, frozen
1 cup	raspberries, frozen
1	banana, sliced
1/3 cup	orange juice
2 cups	vanilla yogurt

Combine everything in a blender.

Process until smooth.

Serve.

This comes in handy at the bakery. Since Katie arrives early, she usually makes a batch when she gets a chance to take a break (of course, she makes enough for Freida, too). This drink is so yummy... and full of gut things, it's a perfect choice for Katie and Freida.

And she shall bring forth a son, and thou shalt call his name Jesus: for he shall save his people from their sins.

- Matthew 1:21

Christmas Cookie Mystery

Katie Chupp felt more than a little guilty as she climbed the ladder . . .
"Dear Lord, please don't let this be something I'll regret. . . please allow *gut* to kumme from it. Let it be a blessing to someone.

In all her seventeen years, she had never taken part in such an activity before, although she had been giving it a lot of thought for some time now. And if she was to be perfectly honest about it, she had wanted the chance to do something about it.

Ach, what would Mamm think if she knew? Would she or Dat approve of what I'm doing right now? Or would they tell me to—

"You're looking awful nervous there, Katie. Are you certain you won't get into all kinds of trouble?"

Katie looked down at Travis Davis, who was holding her ladder steady. Travis had begun working at the Sweet Shop in July, after he returned home to find that his siblings had ransacked the bakery where Katie worked. After insisting that his brothers help to return the bakery to its' pristine condition, Mrs. Simpkins had admonished them to never do such a thing again. Then she had insisted on giving Travis a part-time job at the bakery, until such time that he could find full-time work.Clearing his throat, he continued.

"I don't think your parents would approve. And you might even get in trouble with the church! I'm pretty sure those older dudes who make the rules your family has to follow would frown on this. They might throw you out of the church!" Travis looked troubled, as he held tightly to the ladder.

"*Ach*, that is not going to happen, Travis. You worry too much. If someone from the community finds out, I can always blame it on my rumschpringe." Katie said, stopping halfway up the ladder. She glanced down again at the handsome young man. Katie had caught herself looking at Travis on more than one occasion.

FROSTED CHRISTMAS COOKIES

COOKIES

1 1/2 cups	*white sugar*
1 1/2 cups	*unsalted butter*
2 1/2 teaspoons	*baking powder*
1 teaspoon	*salt*
4 1/2 cups	*all-purpose flour*
2 teaspoons	*pure vanilla extract*
2 teaspoons	*pure almond extract*
2 large	*eggs*

Mix together sugar, butter, shortening, salt and vanilla until smooth and creamy. Add egg. Mix together, scraping sides of bowl. Add flour, mixing only long enough to combine. Divide dough into several balls, each the size of a baseball. Wrap dough in plastic wrap and refrigerate until dough is chilled. Form each ball into a long roll, 1inch in diameter. Refrigerate wrapped dough again until cold.

When ready, preheat oven to 350°F. Remove a roll from the refrigerator and cut into 1/2" thick slices. Place cut side up on a lightly greased cookie sheet. Make indentation in center of each cookie to hold spot of icing.

Bake for 8-10 minutes or until edges begin to slightly turn golden brown. Cool completely on the baking sheet

Frosting recipe on next page

FROSTING

1 1/2 cups	*confectioner's sugar*
1/2 teaspoon	*pure almond extract*
pinch of	*salt*
3-4 tablespoons	*whole milk*

Mix together sugar, almond extract, salt and milk. Continue to add milk 1 tablespoon at a time until icing is desired consistency. Dab a small bit of frosting into each indentation.

GINGER SNAP COOKIES

3/4 cup	shortening
1 cup	white sugar
1 large	egg
1/3 cup	molasses
2 1/3 cups	sifted all-purpose flour
2 teaspoons	baking soda
1 teaspoon	ground ginger
1 teaspoon	ground cinnamon
1/2 teaspoon	ground cloves
1/4 teaspoon	salt
	Extra sugar as needed for dipping

Preheat oven to 350°F. Cream shortening and sugar together. Add molasses and beaten egg. Add spices to sifted flour along with baking soda and salt. Add dry ingredients to creamed mixture. Shape dough into one-inch balls and dip in sugar.

Place on a lightly greased cookie sheet. Bake for 15–18 minutes. Remove from pan and place on rack to cool.

Recipe courtesy of MARILYN RIDGWAY

IRISH SHORTBREAD COOKIES

    1 cup   *unsalted butter*
    2/3 cup   *white sugar*
    1/2 cup   *cornstarch*
    2 cups   *all-purpose flour*

Preheat oven to 275° F. Cream butter and sugar together until light and fluffy. Sift in cornstarch and flour; mix well. Press into 10 ¾ x 7 inch pan. Prick all over with a fork.

Bake for 30 minutes, then reduce heat to 250° F and bake 1 – 1-1/2 hours longer. Remove from pan and sprinkle with powdered sugar. Cut into 20 tube-shaped cookies.

PECAN DROP COOKIES

2 large	*eggs*
3/4 cup	*white sugar*
1 cup	*unsalted butter*
1 cup	*pecans, chopped*
1 teaspoon	*pure vanilla extract*
1/2 teaspoon	*pure almond extract*
2 cups	*all-purpose flour*
1/4 teaspoon	*baking powder*
1/2 teaspoon	*salt*

Preheat oven to 350° F. Combine flour, salt, and baking powder. Mix butter and sugar at high speed until light and fluffy. Add egg, and mix until well blended. Add vanilla extract. Reduce mixer speed to low. Add flour mixture; mix just until combined. Stir in pecans. Shape dough into a 4-inch round balls and cover with plastic wrap. Chill for 1 hour.

Roll dough to 1/4 inch thickness on a lightly floured surface. Cut out 40 (2 x 3 inch) cookies, re-rolling scraps as necessary. Place cookies 1 inch apart on a baking sheet lined with parchment paper.

Bake for 9-10 minutes or until lightly browned on bottoms. Cool on a wire rack. Dust cooled cookies with powdered sugar.

Recipe courtesy of JC MORROWS

CHRISTMAS DATE COOKIES
(kid-friendly recipe)

2 large	eggs
4 cups	rice cereal
1 1/2 cups	chopped dates
1 tablespoon	unsalted butter
2 cups	white sugar
1 bag	coconut (optional)

Add eggs, dates, butter and sugar to medium pot. Cook together 5-15 minutes or until the mixture pulls away from the pan. Pour over rice cereal. Roll into balls and coat with coconut (optional).

Recipe courtesy of LEONA CROUCH

GINGERBREAD COOKIES

1/2 cup	unsalted butter
1/2 cup	white sugar
1/2 cup	brown sugar
1/4 cup	molasses
1 large	egg
2 cups	flour
1/2 teaspoon	ground cinnamon
2 teaspoons	ground ginger
1/4 teaspoon	ground cloves

Cream butter and brown sugar together. Stir in molasses, then egg. In separate bowl, mix flour with spices. Stir in butter/sugar mix. If mixture is too moist, add 1 tablespoon or more flour. Knead dough lightly, then chill for 40 minutes.

Shape dough using cookie cutter of your choice. Bake at 350° F for 10-12 minutes

Recipe courtesy of RACHEL L. MILLER

HOLIDAY SNICKERDOODLES

1 cup	shortening
2 large	eggs
1 1/2 cups	white sugar
2 3/4 cups	all-purpose flour
2 teaspoons	cream of tartar
1 teaspoon	soda
2 tablespoons	colored sugar sprinkles
1 teaspoon	cinnamon

Preheat oven to 350° F. Mix together each color of sugar sprinkles and cinnamon. Set aside for later. Cream together shortening, eggs and sugar. Add flour, cream of tartar and baking soda. Roll mixture into 1-inch to 2-inch balls (depending on what size cookie you want). Roll each ball in a mixture of colored sugar sprinkles and cinnamon.

Bake for 10–12 minutes. Cool on wire rack.

Recipe courtesy of MARILYN RIDGWAY

CHRISTMAS FUDGE
(kid-friendly recipe)

2 cups	creamy peanut butter
2 cups	confectioner's sugar
2 tablespoons	butter, melted
1/2 tablespoon	pure vanilla extract
1/2 tablespoon	pure almond extract

Line a square baking pan with wax paper (8x8 works best). Mix ingredients together. Spread out on the baking pan. Refrigerate for 1 hour (or until hard). Cut into small squares.

Enjoy!

> ** For extra flavor, add 1/2 cup semi sweet chocolate chips, just before time to spread mixture out in the baking pan.
>
> Recipe courtesy of MACY MORROWS

SALTED CARAMEL PEANUT BUTTER KISSES

24	vanilla caramels
1/2 cup	unsalted butter, softened
3/4 cup	creamy peanut butter
1/3 cup	white sugar
1/3 cup	light brown sugar, packed
1 large	egg
2 tablespoons	milk
1 teaspoon	pure vanilla extract
1-1/2 cups	all-purpose flour
1 teaspoon	baking soda
1/2 teaspoon	salt
	ground sea salt

Preheat oven to 350° F. Using hot knife, cut caramels in half. Mix butter and peanut butter until well blended. Add sugars; beat until fluffy. Add egg, milk and vanilla; mix well. Stir together flour, baking soda and salt. Gradually add flour mixture, mixing thoroughly.

Refrigerate for at least 1 hour. Shape dough into 1-inch balls.

Bake 8-10 minutes or until lightly browned. Immediately press a caramel piece into center of each cookie. Sprinkle with sea salt. Return to oven for 1-2 minutes. Remove from cookie sheet to wire rack. Cool completely.

FESTIVE SUGAR COOKIES

1 cup	unsalted butter, softened
1 1/2 cups	white sugar
2 large	eggs
1 teaspoon	pure vanilla extract
1 teaspoon	pure almond extract
2 1/2 cups	all-purpose flour
1/2 teaspoon	baking powder
1/2 teaspoon	salt

Preheat oven to 350° F. Line cookie sheets with parchment paper.

Cream together butter and sugar until light and fluffy, about 3 minutes. Add egg and mix until well-combined. Stir in flour, baking powder, salt, and vanilla. Scoop cookie dough by the tablespoon full and roll into a ball. Place cookie dough onto baking sheet, spacing about 1½-inches to 2 inches apart. Lightly press each cookie down.

Bake for 8-10 minutes or until lightly browned.

Note: When cookies are cool, feel free to decorate—or not.

If you add frosting, set cookies aside to allow it to dry completely. Store in tightly covered container (wax paper between layers) up to 2 weeks.

IRISH GINGERBREAD COOKIES

3 tablespoons	unsalted butter
3 tablespoons	dark brown sugar*
3 tablespoons	white sugar
1 large	egg yolk
1/2 tablespoon	pure vanilla extract
1/2 tablespoon	pure almond extract
1/3 cup	all-purpose flour
1/3 teaspoon	baking powder
1/4 teaspoon	baking soda
1/3 teaspoon	ground cinnamon
1/8 teaspoon	salt
1/2 cup	quick-cook oats (Katie prefers steel cut)

Preheat the oven to 350° F. Line a cookie sheet with parchment paper. Cream together the butter and sugars (with an electric mixer). Add egg yolk and mix until combined. Add vanilla and almond extract and mix. Sprinkle the flour, baking powder, baking soda, cinnamon and salt over the mixture. Mix until combined. Stir in the oats.

Scoop heaping tablespoons of dough and lightly roll into balls. Bake for 10-12 minutes. Let cookies cool completely on cookie sheet. Makes about 1 dozen cookies.

You may store in an air-tight container for up to 3 days.

Recipe courtesy of RACHEL L MILLER

NOTE

The flavor of dark brown sugar really shines in this recipe. If you only have light brown sugar, you can add extra molasses. Per 1 cup of light brown sugar, stir in 1 tablespoon of molasses (Do not use 1 cup in this recipe. Save the excess for use in a later recipe).

Also. . . you'll notice we put the recipe Mrs. Simpkins actually used in the book. . . not the one Mr. O'Neal remembers his dear sweet Grandmother making all those years. Since he cannot actually remember just how much Irish whiskey she put in the recipe, Mrs. Simpkins did a bit of experimenting to come up with this recipe. Also, since Mrs. Simpkins does not drink, she asked Travis to look up a suitable substitution—which he found online.

IRISH SALTED CHOCOLATE COOKIES

COOKIES

1 cup	unsalted butter, softened
1/3 cup	white sugar
1/3 cup	brown sugar
1 teaspoon	pure vanilla extract
1 teaspoon	pure almond extract
2 cups	plain flour

Preheat oven to 350° F. Cream the butter, white sugar and brown sugar together. Add the vanilla and almond extracts and blend together. Slowly add flour, mix. Roll dough into 24 balls. Place on lined baking sheet. Using a spoon, press down to flatten cookie and make little crater for filling.

Bake 10-12 minutes. After removing from oven, use spoon if you desire deeper crater in cookie. Cool cookies on baking sheet for a few minutes. Place cookies, still on lined paper, on a rack to cool.

FILLING

11 ounces	vanilla caramels
3 tablespoons	heavy whipping cream
1 teaspoon	pure vanilla extract
1 teaspoon	pure almond extract
	ground sea salt

Melt caramels and cream, over medium-low heat, stirring constantly. Remove filling from heat and add vanilla and almond extracts. Fill the crater of each cookie with caramel. If desired, sprinkle cookies with ground sea salt.

Recipe contributed by JC MORROWS

NOTE
This recipe originally calls for Irish Whiskey, but when Mr. O'Neal told Mrs. Simpkins he would never touch alcohol again, she improvised, substituting the vanilla and almond flavoring for it.

A soft answer turneth away wrath: but grievous words stir up anger.

- Proverbs 15:1

Lemon Tart Mystery

Thursday started out as a normal day for Katie Chupp. As always, she left home just before sunrise, heading toward the small town located not far from her family's farm.

Katie was eager to get to work, where she would create the most delicious breads, cakes, cookies, and assorted pastries that could be found in Abbott Creek.

When she arrived at The Sweet Shop, it was dark inside. Katie pulled out her key, unlocked the door and stepped inside. After locking the door behind her, she turned on the overhead lights and headed to the kitchen. Comfortable with her daily routine, she went to work, pulling out the ingredients she needed to make nine-grain bread.

Using the large, commercial mixer, she was careful to add everything in the correct order, watching until the dough pulled away from the hooks enough to begin the next step. Then she changed the setting so it would knead the dough until it was ready to knead by hand. She was thankful that the professional mixer did such a gut job and that it spared her much time, but the dough still required a human touch to prepare properly.

Sticking to her routine, she knew precisely what to do. Many mornings found her praying or singing as her hands flattened and pounded dough for one of a dozen breads she baked daily.

Soon she was scraping the dough from the large bowl and working it with her hands on the large countertop. As she squeezed and pressed the dough, flipping the large mound over and repeating her motions again and again, her mind wandered and she thought about how different it was making bread at The Sweet Shop than it was when she baked bread at home.

When making bread for her family, she did every step by hand, mixing and kneading the dough by hand from the very beginning. Even with so many growing *buwes*, their family rarely used more than ten loaves of bread in any given week.

KATIE'S TRIPLE LEMON COOKIES

COOKIES

1 cup	*butter*
1 cup	*sugar*
2	*eggs*
2 tsp	*lemon peel, grated*
1 tbsp	*evaporated milk*
2 1/2-3 cups	*cups self-rising flour*
1/2 cup	*sour lemon drops, crushed*

Preheat oven to 350°F. Cream the butter and sugar together. Add beaten egg, evaporated milk, and lemon peel. Combine the flour and crushed lemon drops; mix with other ingredients. Spread on a greased baking sheet. Bake for 20 minutes. Cool before removing to wire rack.

ICING

1 cup	*confectioner's sugar*
1 tsp	*lemon flavoring*
1 tsp	*water*

Prepare icing, mixing small amounts of confectioners sugar with milk to desired consistency. Spread onto cooled cupcakes.

LEMON SURPRISE CUPCAKES

CUPCAKES

1	lemon supreme cake mix
3 large	eggs
2 tsp	lemon peel, grated
3/4 cup	water
1/3 cup	unsweetened applesauce
1 1/2 cups	blueberries, fresh
1 tbsp	all-purpose flour

Preheat oven to 350°F. Grease and lightly flour 2 cupcake pans (making 24 cupcakes). Set aside. Using a mixer on low speed, blend the cake mix, eggs, and water a few minutes until smooth and creamy. Add lemon zest. Stir lightly until combined. Spoon batter evenly into cupcake pans just over halfway. Toss half the blueberries with a tablespoon of flour. Push 3-4 blueberries into the center of each cupcake. Cover with remaining cake batter. Bake for 15-18 minutes or until a toothpick inserted in the cupcake comes out clean. (Be careful not to insert toothpick into center of cupcake where blueberries are). Remove from the oven and allow to cool before frosting.

ICING

3 1/2 cups	confectioners' sugar
1-2 tbsp	water (additional if needed)
1 tsp	lemon extract

Using a fork, combine confectioners' sugar, 1 tablespoon water, and lemon extract. Add additional tablespoons of water to thin out, if desired. Evenly cover the tops of the cupcakes with frosting. Top each cupcake with three blueberries

KATIE'S LEMON TARTS

TARTS

1 1/2 cups	flour
1 tbsp	sugar
1/4 tsp	salt
1/2 cup	butter, chilled
1/4 cup	ice water

Preheat oven to 375°F. Mix together flour, sugar and salt. Add butter, using a pastry blender or fork (do not over blend). Sprinkle water on the flour mixture, a tbsp at a time, gently mixing with fork until all dough holds together. Form into ball. Let stand several minutes. Roll out dough onto lightly floured surface until thin. Cut in 5" circles (makes 8 tart shells). Fit over inverted custard cups. Pinch together at 4 corners. Prick each tart with fork. Bake for 10-12 minutes.

FILLING

3	yolks
1 cup	sugar
6 tbsp	cornstarch
2 cups	water
1/2 cup	lemon juice
1/4 tsp	salt
3 tbsp	butter
2 tsp	lemon peel, grated

Mix sugar and cornstarch in saucepan over low heat. Stir in water. In small bowl, mix lemon juice and egg yolks together. Beat with fork until well blended. Add to sugar mixture. Stir in salt. Cook over medium heat, stirring constantly, until it thickens. Continue to cook for 2-3 minutes. Remove from heat. Add butter and grated lemon peel. Stir to blend. Cool for one hour, then spoon onto cooled tart shells. Top with fresh blueberries.

ZESTY LEMON BARS

CRUST

1 1/4 cups	all-purpose flour
1/2 cup	butter
1/2 cup	white sugar
2 tsp	lemon peel, grated

Preheat oven to 350°F. In large bowl, beat together butter, sugar and lemon peel. Gradually stir in flour until mixture forms a soft dough. Spread on bottom of un-greased 13x9 pan. Bake 15 minutes. Remove from oven and let cool.

FILLING

1/4 cup	all-purpose flour
1/4 tsp	baking powder
1 cup	brown sugar
1 cup	chopped walnuts
2 large	eggs
2 tsp	lemon peel, grated

Preheat oven to 350°F. In medium bowl, combine ingredients, then spread over baked crust. Bake 20 minutes. Remove from oven.

GLAZE

1 cup	confectioner's sugar
1 tbsp	butter
2 tbsp	lemon juice

In small bowl, blend softened butter with about 1/3 cup of confectioner's sugar. Add lemon juice and the remaining 2/3 cup of confectioner's sugar. Stir until well blended. Drizzle over hot lemon bars. Allow to cool in the pan. Cut into bars before serving.

SINGING NIGHT LEMONADE

    1 1/2 cups   fresh lemon juice (7 large lemons)
    6 cups   water
    3/4 cup   sugar (to taste)
    2 tbsp   honey (raw works best)

Squeeze lemons or use a juicer until you have 1½ cups of juice. Dissolve sugar in water, stir well. Add honey and stir. Add lemon juice to the mixture. Stir together until well-mixed. Serve chilled or over ice. Refrigerate leftovers (if there are any).

Sing the night away.

IMPORTANT NOTE

The above recipe has been adapted for a 2 quart yield. The amount of lemonade needed for the typical Amish youth singing would be at least ten times the amounts listed above.

ORANGE SUPREME BLISS BARS

BARS

1 box	orange supreme cake mix
3.4 oz	instant vanilla pudding mix
4 large	eggs
1 cup	sour cream
1/2 cup	milk

Preheat oven to 350°F. Mix ingredients in a large bowl until blended well. Pour into greased pans and bake for 20 minutes (or until toothpick inserted in middle comes out clean). Cool on wire racks (be sure to put wax paper under wire racks). Cut into bars.

GLAZE

3 cups	powdered sugar
4 tbsp	orange juice

Mix the ingredients of the glaze until smooth and glassy. Pour slowly over cake bars, allowing glaze to run over sides of each bar. Let stand until the glaze is set. Store in cool, dry place.

KATIE'S LEMON BARS

2 cups	all-purpose flour
1 cup	butter
4 teaspoons	lemon peel, grated
1/4 teaspoon	salt
1/2 cup	confectioners sugar
1 cup	white sugar
3 large	large eggs
1/4 cup	lemon juice
* extra	confectioners sugar

Preheat oven to 350°F. Using a food processor, combine flour, butter, 1 teaspoon lemon peel, salt, and 1/2 cup confectioners sugar. Process until mixture looks like coarse crumbs. Press mixture into greased 13 x 9 baking pan. Bake for 18-20 minutes or until golden brown.

In a medium bowl, combine white sugar, eggs, lemon juice, and 3 teaspoons lemon peel. Beat with mixer on medium speed until blended. Pour over warm crust and return to oven. Bake for 18-20 minutes again until golden brown. Remove from oven and place on wire rack. When cool, dust with sifted confectioners sugar. Cut into bars and store at room temperature.

LUSCIOUS LEMON PIE

1 prepared	pie crust
14 ounce can	sweetened condensed milk
8 ounce package	package cream cheese
6 ounce can	lemonade, frozen
1 cup	heavy whipping cream
2 tablespoons	confectioners sugar

Thaw frozen lemonade. Set cream cheese on counter to soften. Combine sweetened condensed milk and softened cream cheese until blended, then add thawed lemonade and lemon juice and mix well to make a creamy lemon filling.

Spoon filling into pie crust and chill until set (several hours). Before serving, combine heavy whipping cream and confectioners sugar with mixer until stiff. Serve pie with freshly whipped topping.

KATIE'S PIE CRUST

2 2/3 cups	sifted all-purpose flour
* plus extra	all-purpose flour, sifted
1 cup	shortening
1 teaspoon	salt
6 tablespoons	ice cold water

Combine flour, shortening, and salt in a large mixing bowl. Cut with pastry cutter. Add water and cut again with pastry cutter.

Sprinkle sifted flour on counter. Divide dough in half and shape into balls. Place one ball of dough on the counter and roll out into large circle (about 12" diameter), adding just enough flour to keep dough from sticking. Carefully place pie crust on pie plate, trim edges, and shape edges if desired. Refrigerate for 20 minutes.

To pre-bake pie crust, preheat oven to 425°F. Place baking sheet in oven. Remove pie crust from refrigerator and pierce bottom of crust several times with fork. Place pie crust on hot baking sheet and bake at 400°F for 20-25 minutes. Cool pie crust before filling.

EASY PINEAPPLE UPSIDE DOWN CAKE

1 box	*yellow cake mix*
1 teaspoon	*pure vanilla extract*
6 tablespoons	*unsalted butter*
7	*fresh pineapple slices in juice*
1/2 cup	*brown sugar*
+ ingredients needed	*for cake mix*

Preheat oven to 350°F. Melt butter in large baking pan or bundt pan. Sprinkle brown sugar evenly over butter. Arrange pineapple slices on brown sugar.

Prepare cake mix according to directions. Add vanilla extract. Pour into pan and bake for 45-55 minutes (or until toothpick inserted in middle comes out clean). Cool on wire rack upright for 15 minutes. Tap pan gently to loosen the cake, invert the pan onto a cake plate and lift off pan. Let cake cool before serving.

KATIE'S EGG CUSTARD PIE

9" unbaked	pie shell
4 large	eggs
2 1/2 cups	milk
1/2 cup	white sugar
1/4 teaspoon	salt
dash	of nutmeg

Preheat oven to 475°F. Mix together eggs, sugar and salt. Heat milk and add to egg mixture. Pour into pie shell. Sprinkle nutmeg over top of pie.

Bake for 5 minutes. Reduce temperature to 425°F. Bake for 10-15 minutes or until completely set. Cool before serving.

EMMA'S HOMEMADE EGG SALAD

6 large	eggs
2 ribs	celery
1/3 cup	mayonnaise
3/4 teaspoon	mustard
1 1/2 tablespoon	pickle relish
1/4 teaspoon	salt
1/4 teaspoon	pepper

Boil eggs for 7 minutes on medium heat. Cool, then peel and chop into small pieces. Dice celery and add to eggs. Mix together in medium bowl the mayonnaise, mustard, pickle relish, salt and pepper. Add additional salt and pepper if needed. Add egg and celery to mixture. Refrigerate until ready to serve.

To every thing there is a season, and a time to every purpose under the heaven...

- Ecclesiastes 3:1

Pumpkin Pie Mystery

Katie looked across the table at her *freinden*. Freida was giggling as Thomas brushed icing off the end of his nose, a half-smile on his face.

Danki, Gott, for bringing mei two freinden together. They are such a wunderbaar couple. Katie wondered how she could have missed Freida's true feelings all this time. They had been *freinden* for many years—ever since they started school together.

However did she keep it from me, her best freind! Why did she never confide in me? Of course, it had been a surprise for everyone. Katie had not been the only one who thought Freida was interested, not in Thomas, but in his outgoing and high-spirited *bruder*.

Timothy's personality simply seemed more suited to Freida's lively and gregarious nature. Everyone had naturally assumed that he would be courting Freida soon.

Thinking of Timothy and Freida together, Katie could see where she had missed an most important piece of the puzzle. Katie had always figured that Timothy was somehow missing Freida's attention. Perhaps it was simply because he was too interested in getting into mischief than paying attention to *maedels*.

Fortunately, Timothy's oblivion had worked in everyone's favor. He had paid no attention to Freida, which had given his *bruder* the courage to take the next step. It had been a surprise to the whole community when the bishop had read the *banns* for Thomas and Freida.

Freida's giggles slowly quieted as Thomas took her hand. A look passed between them that sent a feeling of longing through Katie.

Determined to ignore her sudden melancholy, Katie turned her thoughts to other things. The wedding was less than two weeks away—the day before Thanksgiving—and there was much to be done if they were to be ready on time.

RACHEL'S PUMPKIN PIE

2 cups	fresh pumpkin
2 cups	evaporated milk
1/2 cup	white sugar
2 large	eggs
1 teaspoon	ground cinnamon
1/2 teaspoon	ground ginger
1/2 teaspoon	ground cloves
2 9" unbaked	pie shells

Cut pumpkin in half and remove seeds. Place on cookie sheet (cut side up). Place in oven. Bake at 325°F for 30-45 minutes. Pumpkin peeling will separate while cooking (and pumpkin will soften). Throw away peel.

Preheat oven to 350°F. Mash pumpkin and then measure out 2 cups. Mix together dry ingredients: sugar, cinnamon, ginger and cloves. Break eggs into small bowl and beat before adding to dry mixture. Stir in fresh pumpkin until well blended. Slowly add evaporated milk (the slower, the better).

Pour into thawed pie shells. Don't over-fill. Bake for 45-50 minutes (or until center is set). Cool on wire racks (it slices easier if you wait until it's cool). Cover and refrigerate any remaining pie.

RACHEL'S SWEET POTATO PIE

3 cups	sweet potatoes
1/2 cup	evaporated milk
1 1/4 cups	white sugar
2 large	eggs, beaten
1/2 cup	unsalted butter
2 teaspoons	pure vanilla
2 teaspoons	real maple syrup
2 9" unbaked	pie shells

Preheat oven to 350°F. Peel, slice and boil 3 large or 4 medium sweet potatoes until they are soft enough to mash. In medium bowl, scoop 3 cups mashed potatoes (works best if they're still warm) over butter slices/chunks. Break eggs into small bowl and beat before adding to sweet potatoes. Stir in remaining ingredients one at a time, adding syrup last. Mix thoroughly after each addition.

Pour mixture into thawed pie shells. Bake for 45-50 minutes (or until center is set). Cool on wire racks (it slices easier if you wait until it's cool to cut). Cover and refrigerate any remaining pie.

NAOMI'S HONEY BUTTER

      1 cup   unsalted butter (softened)
4 tablespoons   honey

Blend thoroughly. Enjoy!

I included this recipe because my family and friends always ask for it.
We enjoy it with biscuits, rolls, cornbread, on toast...
Anything goes!

NAOMI'S ROASTED TURKEY

1 large	frozen turkey
1 giant	oval rack roaster (I use a disposable one)
1 turkey size	oven bag
1 tablespoon	flour

Thaw turkey in refrigerator (1 day for every 4 pounds). When ready to cook turkey, remove neck and giblets. Wash turkey thoroughly in cold water. Pat dry. Shake flour in oven bag to coat. Place turkey in oven bag. Close with nylon tie. Cut several slits in top of bag. Place bag in oval rack roaster. Tuck sides of bag in pan.

Bake at 350°F (time will be determined by weight). Bake a 12# turkey for 2 hours, bake a 20# turkey for 2 ½ hours. When done, cut open bag, remove turkey and broth. I usually have several cups of broth to use in gravy, soups, etc. Slice and serve. Pan can be re-used several times.

This is a very simple way to roast a turkey, but many friends and readers ask how I roast my turkey, so I want to include it here—for Thanksgiving. Following the simple directions above, my turkey always turns out tender, moist, and delicious!

I don't have a roaster, so I buy an aluminum throw-away pan and oven bags each year. We roast the turkey, then fix several pans of chex mix... then roast another turkey at Christmas, make more chex mix... and toss the pan.

NAOMI'S HOLIDAY CHEX MIX

INGREDIENTS

3 cups	rice cereal
3 cups	corn cereal
3 cups	wheat cereal
1 1/2 cups	pretzels
1 1/2 cups	bugles

I mix it up, depending on whatever I have on hand. I'll add 1 cup of pretzels, then add 2 more cups of a variety of stuff... bugles, nuts, cheese-its, Ritz crackers, Cheerios, and/or goldfish crackers (just be sure to have 12 cups total). Mix all this in a large bowl.

SEASONING

6 tablespoons	unsalted butter, melted
3 tablespoons	Worcestershire sauce
1 1/2 teaspoons	seasoned salt
3/4 teaspoon	garlic powder
1/2 teaspoon	onion powder

Mix these in a small bowl, then pour carefully over cereal mixture. Bake at 250°F for 1 hour, turning every 15 minutes with a spatula or big wooden spoon.

Store in airtight container.

Enjoy!

IVA'S CORNBREAD DRESSING

STEP 1

3 cups	cornmeal
1 large	egg
1/2	celery stalk
1 medium	onion
*	milk

Preheat oven to 450°F. Dice celery and onion. Mix together cornmeal, egg, and the diced celery and onion. Add enough milk to make a thin or loose batter. Bake in iron skillet for 25 minutes or until done. Let set overnight.

STEP 2

2 large	eggs
1 stick	of unsalted butter
3 teaspoons	sage
*	chicken broth
*	chicken pieces, cooked
*	salt (to taste)
*	pepper (to taste)

Preheat oven to 400°F. Chop cornmeal into pieces. Combine eggs, butter, sage, salt, and pepper. Add cornbread, chicken pieces and enough chicken broth to a stirring consistency.

Pour dressing into large baking dish. Bake for 30-40 minutes or until firm.

RACHEL'S PUMPKIN BREAD

1 1/2 cups	white sugar
4 large	eggs
6 tablespoons	unsalted butter
15 ounce can	pure pumpkin
3/4 cup	whole milk
3 1/2 cups	all-purpose flour
1 teaspoon	baking powder
1 teaspoon	baking soda
1 teaspoon	salt
2 teaspoons	cinnamon
1/2 teaspoon	nutmeg
1/4 teaspoon	ginger
1/4 teaspoon	cloves
1 1/2 cups	pecans, chopped

Preheat oven to 350°F. Grease and flour 2 loaf pans. Cream together sugar and butter until smooth. Add eggs and beat until light and fluffy. Add pumpkin and milk.

Stir together flour, baking powder, baking soda, salt, spices and pecans. Combine dry ingredients and pumpkin mixture; stir until ingredients are moistened. Pour into loaf pans. Tap on counter to settle dough.

Bake for 55-60 minutes (or until center is set). Cool on wire racks for 5-10 minutes. Turn out onto rack to finish cooling. Brush melted butter over tops of pumpkin bread. Wrap in plastic wrap to retain freshness.

You can also bake this bread in small, individual size loaf pans (bake for 45 minutes). These are great idea for gifts.

CRANBERRY PUMPKIN BREAD

2 1/4 cups	*all-purpose flour*
1 1/2 cups	*white sugar*
2 large	*eggs*
1/2 cup	*cranberries (fresh, frozen, or dried)*
6 tablespoons	*unsalted butter*
1 3/4 cups	*pure pumpkin*
2 teaspoons	*baking powder*
1/2 teaspoon	*salt*
2 teaspoons	*cinnamon*
1/2 teaspoon	*nutmeg*
1/4 teaspoon	*ginger*
1/4 teaspoon	*cloves*

Preheat oven to 350°F. Grease and flour 2 loaf pans. Combine flour, baking powder, salt, and spices. Cream together sugar, eggs, butter and pumpkin until smooth. Add pumpkin mixture to flour mixture; stir until moistened. Fold in cranberries. Pour batter into prepared loaf pans. Tap on counter to settle dough.

Bake for 55-60 minutes (or until center is set). Cool on wire racks for 5-10 minutes. Turn out onto rack to finish cooling. Brush melted butter over tops of pumpkin bread. Wrap in plastic wrap to retain freshness.

You can also bake this bread in small, individual size loaf pans (bake for 45 minutes). These are great idea for gifts.

MARTHA'S SAUSAGE BALLS

2 pounds	regular sausage
1 1/4 cups	all-purpose baking mix
4 cups	cheddar cheese, shredded
1/4 cup	finely chopped onion
1/4 cup	finely chopped celery
1/4 cup	garlic powder

Preheat oven to 350°F. Finely chop onion and celery. Mix all ingredients together and form into balls.

Bake for 15 minutes on ungreased cookie sheet until golden brown.

These simple treats can be prepared ahead of time during special events. Mix the ingredients together and form into balls, then freeze. When ready, thaw for 30 minutes, bake and enjoy!

RACHEL'S SWEET POTATO CASSEROLE

1 1/2 cups	sweet potatoes
1/4 cup	brown sugar
1/4 cup	orange juice
1	large egg, beaten
1/4 cup	unsalted butter, melted
1 teaspoon	pure vanilla
1 teaspoon	ground cinnamon
1/4 teaspoon	ground nutmeg
1 teaspoon	real maple syrup
3 cups	miniature marshmallows

Preheat oven to 350°F. Peel, slice and boil 2-3 medium sweet potatoes until they are soft enough to mash. In medium bowl, scoop 1 1/2 cups mashed potatoes (works best if they're still warm) over butter slices/chunks. Break egg into small bowl and beat before adding to sweet potatoes. Stir in remaining ingredients one at a time, adding syrup last. Mix thoroughly after each addition.

Pour mixture into large baking dish. Bake for 18-20 minutes. Top with marshmallows and continue to bake until marshmallows are lightly browned.

> If you don't have time to prepare sweet potatoes, you can substitute with canned yams, although the taste won't be quite as good.

PUMPKIN PECAN PANCAKES

1 1/2 cups	all-purpose flour
1 teaspoon	baking powder
1/2 teaspoon	salt
1 large	egg
1 cup	whole milk
1/2 cup	pure pumpkin
2 tablespoons	white sugar
1/4 teaspoon	ground cinnamon
* pinch of	ground nutmeg
* pinch of	ground ginger
1 cup	pecans, chopped
*	butter or oil (for cooking)

Combine all of the ingredients except pecans and butter; stir until blended. Lightly butter hot griddle and pour 1/4 cup batter for each pancake. Sprinkle with chopped pecans. When bubbles break around the edges, it's time to flip pancake over. Cook until brown on each side. Serve hot with syrup of your choice.

PUMPKIN ORANGE COOKIES

STEP 1

2 1/2 cups	all-purpose flour
1/2 teaspoon	baking soda
1/2 teaspoon	salt
1/2 cup	brown sugar
1 cup	white sugar
1 cup	unsalted butter
1 large	egg
24 ounces	pure pumpkin
2 tablespoons	orange juice
1 teaspoon	orange peel, grated

Preheat oven to 375°F. Combine flour, baking soda and salt in a bowl. Cream white sugar, brown sugar and butter in a large mixing bowl. Add pumpkin, orange juice, orange peel and egg to sugar mixture; beat for 2 minutes. Drop rounded spoonfuls of dough onto an ungreased cookie sheet.

Bake for 12-14 minutes. Remove from oven and transfer cookies to wire racks to cool.

STEP 2

1 1/2 cups	confectioners sugar
2-3 tablespoons	orange juice
1/2 teaspoon	orange peel, grated

Combine ingredients in a medium bowl and beat until smooth. Drizzle over cookies. Be sure to allow time for icing to harden before serving.

*And now abideth faith, hope, charity, these three;
but the greatest of these is charity.*

- 1 Corinthians 13:13

Chocolate Truffle Mystery

Monday morning began just like any other Monday—with one exception. Valentine's Day was two days away and there was much to be done if the Sweet Shop was to be ready on time.

Over the past two weeks, Katie Chupp, with the help of her co-worker Gwen Davis, had been baking more and more special treats for the upcoming holiday, most of which were quickly snapped up by the residents of Abbott Creek.

Orders had been coming in for cookies, cakes, and candies. There were almost as many orders as they had prepared for Christmas. Katie was especially thankful that she had a willing—and helpful—assistant.

Danki Gott, for bringing the Davis family to our community. Gwen is such a blessing to me. I don't know what I would have done the past couple of months without her help. Please bless her family with gut health, supply their needs, and keep them safe.

Only a moment or two after Katie had finished her prayer and went back to work, Travis Davis opened the back door and walked in.

"Hiya, Katie-girl. Hey, Gwennie."

"Gudemariye, Travis."

"Hey, big brother. I'm almost ready to go."

"Good. You don't want to be late to school," he teased his younger sister.

"Katie, I'll come back to pick up the morning deliveries after I drop off Gwen. See ya in a bit."

"Allrecht."

KATIE'S TRIPLE CHOCOLATE CAKE

2 cups	all-purpose flour (sifted)
1 teaspoon	salt
1/2 cup	shortening
1 1/2 cups	white sugar
2 large	eggs
1/2 cup	ice water
1/2 cup	cocoa
1 cup	hot coffee
1 teaspoon	baking soda
1/2 cup	boiling water
2 ounces	dark chocolate

Sift together the flour and salt. Set aside. Add sugar to shortening until creamy Blend in unbeaten eggs. Combine hot coffee and cocoa. Stir to dissolve cocoa. Add to sugar/shortening mixture. Add dry ingredients, blending thoroughly. Dissolve soda in water and add to batter. Grease and lightly flour two 8" cake pans. Pour batter into cake pans.

Bake in pre-heated oven for 30-35 at 375°F. Cakes should be allowed to cool before icing. Shave dark chocolate, using vegetable peeler. After spreading chocolate icing over cake and between layers, cover top of cake with chocolate shavings.

Note. Also makes 30 cupcakcs. Bake 18-22 minutes.

ANDREW'S BANANA BREAD

2 cups	all-purpose flour (sifted)
3/4 cup	white sugar
1/2 cup	butter, softened
1/4 cup	whole milk
1 teaspoon	pure vanilla extract
1 teaspoon	baking soda
1/2 teaspoon	salt
1/2 cup	walnuts, chopped
2 large	eggs
3	ripe bananas, mashed

Cream together sugar, butter, and eggs. Add milk and vanilla. Peel bananas and mash to whatever consistency you prefer. Mix flour, baking soda and salt together. Fold in chopped nuts. Grease and lightly flour loaf pan. Pour batter into cake pans. Bake in pre-heated oven for 55-60 minutes at 350°F.

Cool in the pan for 10 minutes, then set on cooling rack for another 10 minutes before slicing.

KATIE'S CHOCOLATE TRUFFLES

8 ounces	semisweet baking chocolate
1/2 cup	unsweetened cocoa powder
1/2 cup	heavy whipping cream
1 tablespoon	unsalted butter
1 teaspoon	pure vanilla extract

Melt baking chocolate in saucepan over low heat. Stir in butter until melted. Stir in whipping cream and vanilla extract. It should resemble the texture of pudding. If needed, add a few drops of evaporated milk until desired consistency. Refrigerate mixture 15-20 minutes (or until thick enough to shape into balls). Scoop out small balls using a melon baller or spoon. Using gloves, roll balls around in the palms of your hands and place on cookie sheet.

Refrigerate truffles 15-20 minutes until firm. Choose one or more options below to finish. Store in airtight container.

> Option 1. Roll truffles in cocoa powder.
> Option 2. Roll truffles in chopped nuts.
> Option 3. Dip truffles in melted chocolate.

IVA'S RED VELVET CAKE

COOKIES

2 1/4 cups	all-purpose flour (sifted)
1 teaspoon	salt
1/2 cup	shortening
1 1/2 cups	sugar
2 ounces	red food coloring
2 large	eggs
1 cup	buttermilk
2 tablespoons	cocoa
1 teaspoon	pure vanilla extract
1 teaspoon	baking soda
1 tablespoon	vinegar

Cream together shortening, sugar and eggs. Mix food coloring and cocoa. Add to wet mixture. Add salt, flour, buttermilk and vanilla. Gently blend in baking soda and vinegar. Grease and lightly flour three 8" cake pans. Pour batter into cake pans. Bake in pre-heated oven for 30 minutes at 350°F. Cakes should be allowed to cool before icing. Spreading cream cheese frosting between layers and, if desired, over top of cake.

IVA'S CREAM CHEESE FROSTING

8 ounces	cream cheese
8 tablespoons	unsalted butter
4 cups	confectioners sugar
2 teaspoons	pure vanilla extract

Let cream cheese soften to room temperature. And let butter soften to room temperature. Blend cream cheese and butter until smooth. Add pure vanilla and blend well. Stir in confectioners' sugar. Beat until smooth.

Note. In Katie's opinion, this is the best frosting to use not only for Red Velvet Cakes, but also for Carrot Cakes and Pumpkin Cakes.

KATIE'S SUPER HOT CHOCOLATE

6 cups	*nonfat dry milk*
11 ounces	*dry coffee creamer*
16 ounces	*confectioners sugar*
16 ounces	*cocoa powder*

Mix ingredients together and store in an airtight container. To prepare hot chocolate, add 1/2 cup to mug. Add hot water.

* marshmallows are optional :)

KATIE'S NEVER FAIL FUDGE

2 cups	white sugar
1/2 cup	unsalted butter
1/8 teaspoon	salt
2/3 cup	evaporated milk
12 regular size	marshmallows
1 cup	semi-sweet chocolate chips
1 cup	walnuts, chopped
1 teaspoon	pure vanilla extract

Using a 2-quart saucepan, combine sugar, butter, salt, evaporated milk and marshmallows. Cook over medium heat, stirring constantly, until mixture comes to a boil. Let boil for 5 minutes, stirring constantly. Remove from heat.

Stir in chocolate chips, walnuts and vanilla, until completely melted. Spread into a buttered 8" square pan. Allow to cool before cutting into small, square pieces.

OHIO'S BUCKEYE CANDY

1 1/2 cups	creamy peanut butter
4 cups	confectioners sugar
1 stick	unsalted butter
1 teaspoon	pure vanilla extract
16 ounces	semi-sweet chocolate
1/4 cup	paraffin

Begin melting paraffin and chocolate chips in a small crockpot. Melt butter. Add peanut butter, vanilla and sugar. Shape into small balls. Cool in freezer. Use toothpick to dip each one in the melted chocolate. Cool on wax paper. Store in layers between wax paper.

Note: Stop before dipping candy completely in chocolate to make them look like buckeyes.

MARTHA'S CREAM CHEESE FUDGE

6 ounces	*semi-sweet chocolate chips*
6 ounces	*cream cheese, softened*
4 cups	*confectioners sugar, sifted*
2 teaspoons	*evaporated milk*
1 1/2 teaspoons	*pure vanilla extract*
1/4 teaspoon	*salt*
1 1/2 cups	*nuts, chopped*

Melt chocolate chips using a double-boiler. In a large bowl, beat cream cheese until smooth. Add confectioners sugar and evaporated milk. Stir in melted chocolate into cheese mixture. Add vanilla and salt. Add nuts, if desired.

Press the mixture in a buttered 9" square pan. Cover and refrigerate overnight.

ANDREW'S FAVORITE CHURCH CAKE

1 package	*German chocolate cake mix*
12 ounces	*semi-sweet chocolate chips*
1 cup	*miniature marshmallows*
1/4 cup	*unsalted butter, melted*
1/2 cup	*brown sugar*
1/2 cup	*pecans, chopped*

Preheat oven to 350°F. Grease 2qt baking dish with butter. Prepare cake mix as directed on package. Fold chocolate chips and marshmallows into batter. Pour into prepared baking dish. Drizzle melted butter over batter. Sprinkle with brown sugar and top with nuts.

Bake for 45-50 minutes or until cake is done.

Serve cold... or serve warm with vanilla ice cream.

IVA'S PECAN PIE

3 large	eggs
1 cup	white sugar
1 cup	Karo syrup
1 stick	unsalted butter
1 cup	pecans
1 9"	pie shell

Preheat oven to 350°F. Mix ingredients together and pour into pie shell.

Bake for 55 minutes.

Allow to cool before slicing and serving.

NAOMI'S FAVORITE CARAMEL BARS

STEP 1

1 cup	all-purpose flour
1 cup	quick oats
3/4 cup	light brown sugar
1/2 teaspoon	baking soda
1/8 teaspoon	salt
3/4 cup	unsalted butter
1 cup	chocolate chips

Melt butter; set aside. Preheat oven to 350°F. Grease 9x13 baking dish with butter. Combine flour, oats, brown sugar, baking soda and salt. Stir in melted butter; mix well.

Press into prepared dish and bake for 10 minutes or until set. Sprinkle chocolate chips over top.

STEP 2

12 ounces	caramel ice cream topping
1 tablespoon	all-purpose flour

Stir together caramel and flour. Drizzle over chocolate chips. Bake for 20 minutes or until bubbly. Cool completely before cutting. Cut into 36 squares.

*...choose you this day whom ye will serve
...as for me and my house, we will serve the Lord.*

- Joshua 24:15

Peach Cobbler Mystery

Friday morning began the same as most Fridays, with Katie driving in to work with her *Englisch* boyfriend. She loved starting the day with Travis, who would usually regale her with stories of his family

"And Bobby declared that he was getting older and wants to be called 'Bob' from now on." Travis said.

"Gwen told him he would always be Bobby to her. He yelled, then he smacked his hand on the table and said that maybe she can call him Bobby at home, but that she had better not call him that at school. Of course, he got angry and ran outside when we all started laughing."

"That's so cute! I don't remember Ervin, Noah or Caleb ever doing that. Of course, their names are harder to shorten." Katie laughed, then she asked, "is Bobby's legal name Bob?"

"No, it's not Bob. And it's not Robert." Travis answered, laughing. "His legal name actually is Bobby."

Katie's laughter mixed with his. She loved how easily they could talk about family, life at home, their work and people they knew.

"Oh my goodness. I would never have guessed. I always thought Bobby was a nickname." Katie said with a smile.

"He can use Bob as a nickname, but I think he's gonna need to get over being called Bobby." Travis looked thoughtful. "I guess Mom needs to show him his birth certificate and explain it to him before there's any trouble."

KATIE'S PEACH COBBLER

1 cup	*self-rising flour*
1 cup	*white sugar*
2 cups	*peaches, sliced*
1/2 cup	*unsalted butter*
1 large	*egg*
1 teaspoon	*pure vanilla extract*

Preheat oven to 350°F. Grease 2qt baking dish with butter. Spread sliced peaches in baking dish. Sprinkle 1/2 tablespoon sugar over top of peaches. Blend remaining sugar and softened butter until mixed well. Add flour to mixture. Add egg and vanilla extract. Mix well. Spread batter over tops of peaches.

Bake for 35-40 minutes, until crust is brown. Let stand 10 minutes before serving. Best served with ice cream.

Yield: Serves 12 (or 2 expectant mothers).

KATIE'S BABY SHOWER MINTS

8 ounces	cream cheese, softened
1/2 cup	unsalted butter, softened
2 1/2 cups	confectioners sugar
1 teaspoon	pure mint extract
2-3 drops	pink food coloring
2-3 drops	blue food coloring
2-3 drops	green food coloring
2-3 drops	yellow food coloring

Mix together cream cheese and butter. Add 1 cup of the confectioners sugar. Stir until mixed well. Add mint extract and stir to mix well. Slowly add another cup of confectioners sugar, mixing until smooth and creamy. To make 4 multiple colors, separate dough into 4 bowls. Add 2-3 drops of food coloring to each bowl and mix until desired color. Cover. Refrigerate for several hours.

Line two cookie sheets with wax paper and dust with confectioners sugar. Form dough into 1" balls and roll in the confectioners sugar. Flatten each ball with the tines of a fork. Let stand, uncovered until mints are firm (this will take several hours). Store in airtight container (with wax paper between layers).

Yield: 8 dozen.

KATIE'S PARTY MINTS

1 cup unsalted	butter, softened
32 ounces	confectioners sugar
2 tablespoons	whole milk
2 teaspoon	pure vanilla extract
1 teaspoon	pure mint extract
2-3 drops	pink food coloring
2-3 drops	blue food coloring
2-3 drops	green food coloring
2-3 drops	yellow food coloring

Mix butter and 1 cup confectioners sugar until smooth and creamy. Gradually add remainder of sugar, blending well. Add milk, vanilla extract and mint extract. To make 4 multiple colors, separate dough into 4 bowls. Add 2-3 drops of food coloring to each bowl and mix until desired color.

Line 2 cookie sheets with wax paper. Form dough into 1" balls; place on pan. Flatten each ball with the tines of a fork. Refrigerate until ready to serve.

Yield: 8 dozen

GWEN'S BABY SHOWER CUPCAKES

CAKE

2 cups	cake flour
1 tablespoon	baking powder
1/2 teaspoon	salt
1 cup	white sugar
3 large	egg whites
1 cup	heavy cream
1/2 cup	cold water
1 tablespoon	pure vanilla extract

ICING

2 cups	confectioners sugar
1/2 teaspoon	pure almond extract
4-6 tablespoon	whole milk
* additional	milk as needed

Mix together flour, baking powder, salt and sugar. Using mixer, beat egg whites until slightly stiff. Using mixer, pour cream into another bowl and beat until stiff. Add egg whites and fold together until blended. Stir water and vanilla extract together. Add to cream/egg mixture, gently stirring until blended. Gradually sprinkle onto flour mixture and stir until well blended.

Spoon batter into paper baking cups, filling each cup half full. Bake at 350°F about 15 minutes or until done. Remove from oven and cool. Prepare icing, mixing confectioners sugar with pure almond extract. Add small amounts of milk until icing is desired consistency. Spread over top of cooled cupcake.

Yield: 48 cupcakes.

KATIE'S PEACH PUNCH

16 ounces	frozen peaches
3 fresh	peaches
64 ounces	peach/white grape juice
2 liters	sprite, chilled
1 fresh	lemon
1/2 cup	white sugar
6 scoops	vanilla ice cream

Puree peaches until smooth. Set aside. Add sugar, gelatin and water to saucepan. Bring to boil. Stir until gelatin and sugar dissolve.

Puree frozen peaches, sugar and juice from lemon. Set aside. Pour white grape/peach juice into large punch bowl. Add pureed mixture. Slowly add chilled liter of sprite. Stir well.

Garnish with fresh peach slices.

Yield: Serves 12.

PEANUT BUTTER KRISPIE TREATS

3 tablespoons	*butter*
4 cups	*miniature marshmallows*
6 cups	*rice cereal*
1/2 cup	*creamy peanut butter*

Melt butter in large saucepan over low heat. Add marshmallows and stir until completely melted. Add peanut butter and stir until mixed well. Remove from heat.

Add rice cereal. Stir until well coated. Grease 9x13" baking pan with butter. Using buttered spatula, press mixture into baking pan. When cool, cut into 2" squares.

KATIE'S RICE PUDDING

1 cup	whole milk
1 cup	water
1 cup	rice, uncooked
2 large	eggs
1 cup	evaporated milk
1 teaspoon	pure vanilla extract
1/4 cup	white sugar
1/8 teaspoon	ground cinnamon

Using a 2-quart saucepan, heat milk and water over medium heat. Add rice and bring to boil. Lower the heat, stirring every 10 minutes. Cook uncovered for 30 minutes, or until rice is tender. In a large bowl, combine eggs, 3/4 cup of the evaporated milk, vanilla and sugar. Set aside.

Add the remaining evaporated milk to the rice mixture. Spoon 1 cup of the rice mixture into the egg mixture and stir. Pour the egg/rice mixture into the remaining rice. Heat until it boils, stirring constantly. Remove from heat. Sprinkle with cinnamon.

MARTHA'S COOKED APPLES

5	medium apples
1 tablespoon	fresh lemon juice
1/4 cup	unsalted butter
3/4 cup	brown sugar
3/4 teaspoon	ground cinnamon
1/4 teaspoon	salt
* dash	ground nutmeg

Peel and slice apples. Using a large skillet, combine apples and lemon juice on medium heat. Add butter, brown sugar, cinnamon, salt, and nutmeg. Stir, cover, and cook for 30 minutes or until apples slices are soft.

NAOMI'S 7-LAYER SALAD

1/2	*head of lettuce*
6	*hard-boiled eggs*
1	*small onion*
12 ounce	*can of baby peas*
2 cups	*mayonnaise*
2 cups	*cheddar cheese, shredded*
1 pound	*bacon*

Finely chop onion and saute in butter. Fry bacon, drain, and crush.

Add each ingredient, making individual layers in a large glass bowl.

Layer 1: tear up lettuce and place in bottom of bowl.
Layer 2: chop up hard-boiled eggs.
Layer 3: spread onion over eggs.
Layer 4: drain peas and add to bowl.
Layer 5: Gently spread mayonnaise over peas.
Layer 6: Sprinkle shredded cheese over mayonnaise.

When ready to serve, add layer 7: Sprinkle bacon bits over cheese.

NAOMI'S HONEY MUSTARD

1/4 cup   *mayonnaise*
1 tablespoon   *mustard*
1 tablespoon   *pure honey*
1/2 tablespoon   *lemon juice*

Combine ingredients and whip until well blended.

NAOMI'S GARLIC HERB SPREAD

8 ounces	cream cheese, softened
1/4 cup	parmesan
1/4 cup	mayonnaise
1-2	garlic cloves
1 teaspoon	Italian seasoning
1 tablespoon	parsley

Combine ingredients and whip until well blended.

AMISH WEDDING BROCCOLI CHEESE SOUP

7 pounds	broccoli, chopped
2 pounds	Velveeta cheese
1 quart	sweet whipping cream
1/2 cup	cornstarch
*	cold water

Cook broccoli, adding enough water just to cover it. When broccoli is tender, add Velvet cheese and whipping cream. Stir until cheese is melted and ingredients are mixed. Add corn starch to thicken.

"And Jesus said unto them, I am the bread of life: he that cometh to me shall never hunger; and he that believeth on me shall never thirst."

- John 6:35

THANK YOU

for visiting

Abbott Creek